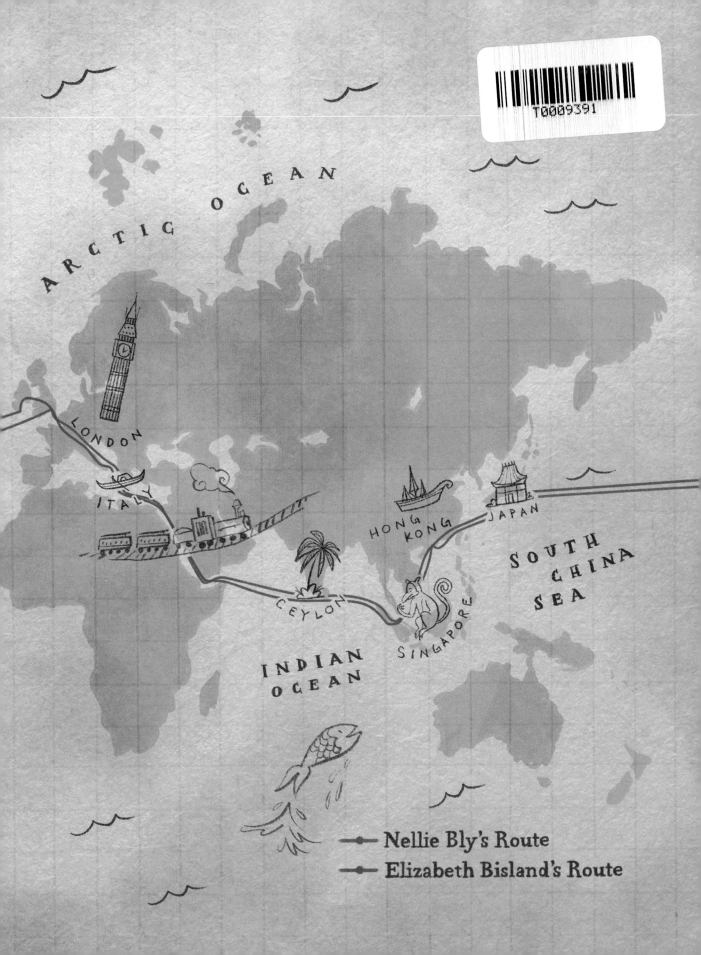

ARCTIC OCEAN

LONDON

ITALY

CEYLON

HONG KONG

JAPAN

SINGAPORE

SOUTH CHINA SEA

INDIAN OCEAN

Nellie Bly's Route
Elizabeth Bisland's Route

A Race Around the World

The True Story of Nellie Bly & Elizabeth Bisland

Caroline Starr Rose

illustrated by Alexandra Bye

Albert Whitman & Company
Chicago, Illinois

The world was awhirl in 1889. Telegraph messages whizzed over wires. Express trains and steamships flew at top speeds. Big cities boasted electrical lights and a talking device called the telephone.

How long would it take to circle this newly speeding world? One travel writer girdled the globe in only a year and a half. An all-star baseball team knocked out the trip in six quick months. Author Jules Verne's fictional hero Phileas Fogg went around the world in eighty days, a trip so amazing it could take place only in the pages of a storybook.

A reporter named Nellie Bly believed she could be even faster.

Nellie loved a challenge.

After studying ship routes and train schedules, she was certain she could travel the world in seventy-five days—a one-woman race against distance and time. The adventure would make a great story.

Her boss at the New York *World* said only a man could manage such a trip. Ladies never traveled alone, and they always packed far too much luggage.

"Very well," Nellie said. "Start the man, and I'll start the same day for some other newspaper and beat him."

"I believe you would," said her boss.

When Nellie finally learned she could go, she had just three days to prepare.

On November 14, 1889, Nellie boarded the *Augusta Victoria* from a New Jersey dock, clutching a single bag. In seventy-five days, she'd be back. She couldn't fail.

In a New York apartment only a few miles away from the docks, Elizabeth Bisland was leisurely reading when a messenger arrived at her door. She was needed at work. Immediately.

Elizabeth's publisher at the *Cosmopolitan* magazine had just read in the paper of Nellie Bly's trip.

"Would you leave New York this evening for San Francisco," he asked Elizabeth, "and continue from there around the world?" He was sure she could beat Nellie.

At first Elizabeth said, "I mean to do nothing of the sort!" She had never left the country before. She had no desire to race Nellie Bly. She was content with her quiet work.

But Elizabeth had always dreamed of traveling the world, visiting the places she'd read of in books. She'd do the job she'd been given.

There were only five hours to prepare before her train left Grand Central.

The race was on!

Elizabeth's train careened west, fierce as a runaway horse.

At daybreak on the second day, she awakened to a world etched with ice crystals.

Sailing for England, Nellie's eastbound steamer lurched and pitched as though light as a juggler's ball. She sat at the ship captain's table, battling seasickness.

Far out at sea, Nellie had no way of knowing that her one-woman dash was now a contest of two.

Exciting news awaited Nellie in England. Author Jules Verne wanted to meet the young lady trying to beat Phileas Fogg, the hero of his book. But Nellie's next stop was supposed to be Italy, and Jules lived in France.

The detour meant two sleepless nights as she took two trains through England, a ferry to France, and yet another train for the brief visit with Jules.

Two *more* train rides later, Nellie reached Italy hours behind schedule. She dashed to the pier, arriving at her ship just in time.

In San Francisco, crowds buzzed with questions for Elizabeth. They jostled to see the brave lady journalist set sail. How excited she was to leave her country for the very first time!

One day from shore, a storm boiled in the Pacific. Waters raged as the ship bucked and groaned.

At last the storm faded. Elizabeth ventured on deck. She was mesmerized with the ocean's depths of sparkling sapphire and shades of violet. There was so much to see, such wonder and beauty. It was like a page from a book—only better.

Nellie arrived in Ceylon two days early—such a satisfying feat! She was the first passenger from her ship to reach shore.

Nellie feasted on fiery curry and lounged in the cool ocean breeze. She took a moonlit ride under arching palms while waves roared on the beach.

Then bad news—Nellie's ship was delayed. Her two-day stopover stretched to five.

Three *more* days stuck in Ceylon! Nellie fretted. She stormed about. Her head pounded furiously.

In the cities of Japan, Elizabeth browsed in shops brimming with porcelain, flowers, fabrics, and jade. She marveled at sloping hills and mist-filled valleys. She wandered temples and tombs as elegant as poetry.

White lanterns swung from jinrickshas, dancing like fireflies. At night, the moon transformed the bay to flowing gold.

Two days in Japan weren't nearly enough. Elizabeth promised herself one day she'd return to the land where Mount Fuji shone like a pearl.

In Singapore, Nellie bought a feisty macaque, which she named McGinty.

In Hong Kong's harbor, Elizabeth was entranced by the glitter of lights and the sampans gliding in the evening mist.

A roaring monsoon battered Nellie's ship.
A steamer with a broken propeller changed Elizabeth's travel plans.

During the third week of December, in the South China Sea,
two steamers passed. One carried Nellie. One Elizabeth.
There was no way to know who was winning.

"The other woman. She is going to win," the man at the steamship office told Nellie when she arrived in Hong Kong. This other woman, he said, had passed through Hong Kong just days before.

Nellie stared at him. What other woman? What could he mean? "It's too bad," he said, "but I think you have lost."

Nellie could hardly believe it! In this moment when time mattered most, she couldn't fall behind. She'd never been beaten. She wouldn't be now.

That night, in a Singapore hotel, a noise startled Elizabeth. Her heart boomed in her chest. A tiger was in her room; she was certain of it!

Boldly, Elizabeth lit a candle.

It wasn't a tiger but an enormous rat, rifling through her stockings and sniffing her gloves. A rat was almost as awful as a tiger, but at least she wouldn't be dinner.

Nellie set sail on the *Oceanic*—the very same steamer that had arrived with Elizabeth just thirteen days before. The chief engineer, so confident in his ship, ordered his men to write on the engines

For Nellie Bly

We'll win or die.

Elizabeth explored the deserts of Aden, astonished at their ancient beauty. Her steamer continued across the Arabian; it skimmed the Red and Mediterranean Seas. Then a train carried her over the snow-covered mountains of Italy and on to France. By the time she arrived, the boat she needed to take had already left.

In San Francisco, Nellie learned that blizzards had stopped the Central Pacific Railroad. No trains would get through for days. It was the worst snow the railroad had ever seen.

Elizabeth hurried to England. Still she missed two other ships. She had one more chance to cross the Atlantic— a final steamer, one train ride away.

Nellie wouldn't let the snow stop her. She and McGinty took a train on the Southern Pacific line instead. The deserts in Arizona and New Mexico flickered past. On Nellie went through Kansas to Chicago, well-wishers gathering at every station. From Indiana to Pennsylvania, crowds swelled with people waving handkerchiefs and hats.

Elizabeth's ship, the *Bothnia*, was one of the slowest in the fleet. The Atlantic Ocean churned with storms, the worst winter in years. Elizabeth was so miserable, she hardly moved from her berth.

In Jersey City, a crowd swarmed, thousands strong.
Train wheels groaned and slowed to a stop.

As Nellie stepped onto the platform, three official timekeepers checked their watches. On January 25, 1890, at 3:51 p.m. and 44 seconds, the great race ended. A ten-cannon salute boomed from Manhattan's Battery Park. Boats up and down the Hudson River whistled in celebration.

72 days, 6 hours, 11 minutes, and 14 seconds. Nellie had beaten her own goal by almost three days. She'd traveled faster than she'd hoped for. Even bested Elizabeth Bisland.

On January 30, Elizabeth stood on deck as New York formed on the horizon.

The Statue of Liberty held her torch high, beckoning the sea-weary travelers. Skyscrapers jutted, their jagged, man-made peaks a world away from Mount Fuji.

Home. It was as though she'd never left.

At 1:30 p.m., the *Bothnia* pulled into a pier in New York Harbor. No official timekeepers awaited. Only a modest crowd had gathered— the race had ended four and a half days earlier. Elizabeth didn't hide her disappointment. For seventy-six days she'd given everything, just to come in second.

Nellie had won! She was famous. She'd shown
everyone she was as daring and capable as any man.
Elizabeth lost, but her journey had only just begun.
She would write and travel for the rest of her days.

NELLIE BLY, BYE AND BYE.

NELLIE BLY
EXTRA

EXTRA
WELCOME
LIE BLY
IVES
CITY

SHE'S BROKEN EVERY RECORD!

28
DAYS

120

146

NEW YORK. FRIDAY JANUARY 10 1890.

MORNING EDITION

World

FATHER TIME
OUTDONE

EVEN IMAGINATION'S RE
PALES BEFORE THE PERFO
OF "THE WORLD'S"
GLOBE CIRCLE

A FLYING TRIP AROUND THE WORLD

A
FLYING TRIP
AROUND
·THE·
WORLD
>IN SEVEN STAGES<
ELIZABETH BISLAND

WELCOME
NELLY BLY ARRIVES HOME SAFELY
JANUARY 25 1890!

YORK
I.S.

In this newly whirling world made swifter by fast trains and steamships, Nellie and Elizabeth's race was an extraordinary feat. Both circled the globe more quickly than any who'd tried before. Both journeyed alone. Both took on the world and triumphed, each on her own terms.

Author's Note

I had a book about Nellie Bly while growing up and thought I knew the essential facts about her famous trip around the world. But it wasn't until I was an adult and started researching Nellie's life that I learned a second woman started her own race just hours after Nellie's. Like Nellie, the woman was a journalist living in New York. Her name was Elizabeth Bisland.

In the 1880s, only two percent of American journalists were women. Most newspapers assigned them to write pieces about fashion, homemaking, or society gossip for separate women's sections—hardly the kinds of stories that would be considered news.

But Nellie Bly insisted her reporting equaled any man's, and she asked for challenging assignments. At New York City's the *World*, her undercover story about the neglectful treatment of the mentally ill led to much-needed reform at city hospitals and asylums.

While Nellie thrived in the bustling newspaper setting, Elizabeth Bisland's joy was literature, and she preferred the more leisurely pace of a monthly magazine. She hosted gatherings in her apartment to discuss the arts and wrote poetry and book reviews.

In 1888, Bly approached her editor at the *World* with an idea: after studying steamship and train schedules, she had determined she could travel the world in seventy-five days—more quickly than the character Phileas Fogg, from Jules Verne's popular novel *Around the World in Eighty Days*. Nellie knew it would make a great story. Recent technological advances like the telegraph and steamship had transformed the world, making it feel both faster and smaller. Things that had been unimaginable just a few years before were possible now.

The day before Nellie set sail, she had a special dress made, one that would be able to withstand three months of continual wear. She also bought an overcoat. Nellie packed everything she considered essential—a few changes of underwear, a dressing gown, a pair of slippers, a traveling cup, pins and needles and thread, paper, an inkstand, and a jar of cold cream—in a small handbag.

Elizabeth Bisland, who was working as the literary editor at the *Cosmopolitan* magazine, was given even shorter notice than the three days Nellie had. When Elizabeth's publisher read of Nellie's departure on the morning of November 14, 1889, he saw a publicity opportunity. The *Cosmopolitan* would send its own lady journalist around the world, changing Nellie's race against distance and time into a race between two women, with Nellie traveling east and Elizabeth traveling west. Seven and a half hours after she was called to the office, Elizabeth's own journey was underway.

The race quickly became an international story. Nellie and Elizabeth sent occasional telegrams back to New York—their only means of direct communication. These brief reports added to the interest and mystery surrounding the race. The *World* ran a contest encouraging readers to guess Nellie's final travel time down to the second, offering a trip to Europe as the grand prize, and in the first week of the contest, the newspaper gained more than 300,000 new subscribers.

Each woman's trip was roughly 28,000 miles. While Nellie was sometimes delayed, she never missed a connection. Even when snow stopped the Central Pacific Railroad, The *World* was able to quickly charter a special train on another line. Elizabeth, however, ran into trouble a number of times. She had to change plans in Hong Kong because of a damaged ship. She missed three steamers while trying to cross the Atlantic Ocean. During the race, both women experienced seasickness, loneliness, storms, and extreme changes in weather. Both found moments to enjoy their surroundings despite their hurried pace.

The more I read about Nellie and Elizabeth, the more it seemed to me that both women won the race, each in her own way. Nellie earned the recognition she longed for, becoming, for a time, the most famous journalist in the world. Elizabeth gained the opportunity to see the places she'd read about in books. Just months after the race, Elizabeth returned to England. There she befriended artists and authors, continued with her writing, and met her husband, who traveled with her when she returned to countries she'd visited years before. Most of the trip they spent in Japan, a country Elizabeth had come to love more than anywhere else in the world.

Twenty-five-year-old Nellie was plucky and quick. Twenty-eight-year-old Elizabeth was thoughtful and reserved. Nellie came up with the idea for the around-the-world trip. Elizabeth had the trip thrust upon her. Nellie is remembered to this day. Elizabeth is largely forgotten to history. Yet both traveled faster than Phileas Fogg, turning his imaginary voyage into a real-life accomplishment, something no one—man or woman—had ever done before.

Selected Sources

Bisland, Elizabeth. I*n Seven Stages: A Flying Trip Around the World*. Harper & Brothers, 1891.

Bly, Nellie, and Jean Marie Lutes. *Around the World in Seventy-Two Days and Other Writings*. Penguin Books, 2014.

Goodman, Matthew. *Eighty Days: Nellie Bly and Elizabeth Bisland's History-Making Race Around the World.* Ballantine Books, 2014.

To my parents, who gave me the world—CSR

To my family, for all the love and adventures—AB

Text copyright © 2019 by Caroline Starr Rose
Illustrations copyright © 2019 by Albert Whitman & Company
Illustrations by Alexandra Bye
First published in the United States of America in 2019 by Albert Whitman & Company
ISBN 978-0-8075-0010-1 (hardcover)
ISBN 978-0-8075-0011-8 (ebook)

Printed in China
10 9 8 7 6 5 4 3 WKT 26 25 24 23 22 21

Design by Ellen Kokontis

For more information about Albert Whitman & Company,
visit our website at www.albertwhitman.com.